Arduino:

The Ultimate Beginner's Guide

Lee Maxwell

© 2016

TABLE OF CONTENT

Introduction

I want to thank you and congratulate you for downloading the book, *Arduino: The Ultimate Beginner's Guide"*.

This book contains proven steps and strategies on how to The root of the Arduino extend began at the Interaction Design Institute Ivrea in Ivrea, Italy. Around then understudies utilized a BASIC Stamp at a cost of $100, considered costly for understudies. In 2004, Colombian understudy Hernando Barragán made the improvement stage Wiring as a Master's theory extend at the Interaction Design Institute Ivrea (IDII) in Ivrea, Italy. Massimo Banzi and Casey Reas, who are known for work on the Processing dialect were chiefs for his postulation. The venture objective was to make ease, straightforward apparatuses for non-designers to make advanced undertakings. The Wiring stage comprised of an equipment PCB with an ATmega168 microcontroller, an IDE in light of Processing and library capacities to effortlessly program the microcontroller.

In 2005, Massimo Banzi, with David Mellis, an IDII , and David Cuartielles, included support for the less expensive ATmega8 microcontroller to Wiring. Be that as it may, rather than proceeding with the work on Wiring, they forked (or replicated) the Wiring source code and began running it as a different venture, called Arduino.

The Arduino's underlying center group comprised of Massimo Banzi, David Cuartielles, Tom Igoe, Gianluca Martino, and David Mellis.

The name Arduino originates from a bar in Ivrea, where a portion of the originators of the venture used to meet. The bar was named after Arduin of Ivrea, who was the margrave of the March of Ivrea and King of Italy from 1002 to 1014.

Taking after the consummation of the Wiring stage, lighter and lower cost renditions were circulated in the open-source group.

Equipment

This present area's authentic exactness might be traded off due to outdated data. If it's not too much trouble redesign this article to reflect late occasions or recently accessible data. (October 2015)

This area needs extra references for check. If you don't mind enhance this article by adding references to solid sources. Unsourced material might be tested and evacuated. (May 2013) (Learn how and when to evacuate this format message)

Arduino-perfect R3 UNO board made in China with no Arduino logo, yet with indistinguishable markings, including "Made in Italy" content

Arduino is open-source equipment. The equipment reference plans are conveyed under a Creative Commons Attribution Share-Alike 2.5 permit and are accessible on the Arduino site. Format and generation records for a few variants of the equipment are likewise accessible. The source code for the IDE is discharged under the GNU General Public License, form 2. By the by an official Bill of Materials of Arduino sheets has never been discharged by the staff of Arduino.

Thanks again for downloading this book, I hope you enjoy it!

Chapter 1

What is Arduino?

Arduino is an open-source gadgets stage in view of simple to-utilize equipment and programming. Arduino sheets can read inputs - light on a sensor, a finger on a catch, or a Twitter message - and transform it into a yield - actuating an engine, turning on a LED, distributing something on the web. You can advise your board what to do by sending an arrangement of guidelines to the microcontroller on the board. To do as such you utilize the Arduino programming dialect (in light of Wiring), and the Arduino Software (IDE), in view of Processing.

Throughout the years Arduino has been the mind of a huge number of tasks, from regular items to complex logical instruments. An overall group of creators - understudies, specialists, craftsmen, software engineers, and experts - has assembled around this open-source stage, their commitments have signified an unbelievable measure of available information that can be of awesome help to amateurs and specialists alike.

Arduino was conceived at the Ivrea Interaction Design Institute as a simple device for quick prototyping, went for understudies without a foundation in hardware and programming. When it achieved a more extensive group, the Arduino board began changing to adjust to new needs and difficulties, separating its offer from straightforward 8-bit sheets to items for IoT applications, wearable, 3D printing, and implanted situations. All Arduino sheets are totally open-source, engaging clients to fabricate them freely and in the long run adjust them to their specific needs. The product, as well, is open-source, and it is becoming through the commitments of clients around the world.

Why Arduino?

On account of its basic and available client encounter, Arduino has been utilized as a part of a huge number of various tasks and applications. The Arduino programming is anything but difficult to-use for learners, yet sufficiently adaptable for cutting edge clients. It keeps running on Mac, Windows, and Linux. Instructors and understudies utilize it to assemble minimal effort logical instruments, to demonstrate science and material science standards, or to begin with programming and mechanical autonomy. Creators and draftsmen manufacture intelligent models, artists and specialists utilize it for establishments and to explore different avenues regarding new melodic instruments. Producers, obviously, utilize it to construct large portions of the undertakings displayed at the Maker Faire, for instance. Arduino is a key device to learn new things. Anybody - youngsters, specialists, craftsmen, developers - can begin tinkering simply taking after the well ordered directions of a pack, or offering thoughts online to different individuals from the Arduino people group.

There are numerous different microcontrollers and microcontroller stages accessible for physical registering. Parallax Basic Stamp, Netmedia's BX-24, Phidgets, MIT's Handyboard, and numerous others offer comparable usefulness. These apparatuses take the muddled points of interest of microcontroller programming and wrap it up in a simple to-utilize bundle. Arduino additionally improves the way toward working with microcontrollers, however it offers some favorable position for educators, understudies, and intrigued beginners over different frameworks:

• Inexpensive - Arduino sheets are generally reasonable contrasted with other microcontroller stages. The slightest costly variant of the Arduino module can be collected by hand, and even the pre-gathered Arduino modules cost under $50

• Cross-stage - The Arduino Software (IDE) keeps running on Windows, Macintosh OSX, and Linux working frameworks. Most microcontroller frameworks are restricted to Windows.

• Simple, clear programming environment - The Arduino Software (IDE) is anything but difficult to-use for tenderfoots, yet sufficiently adaptable for cutting edge clients to exploit also. For educators, it's advantageously in light of the Processing programming environment, so understudies figuring out how to program in that environment will be acquainted with how the Arduino IDE functions.

• Open source and extensible programming - The Arduino programming is distributed as open source devices, accessible for expansion by experienced software engineers. The dialect can be extended through C++ libraries, and individuals needing to comprehend the specialized subtle elements can make the jump from Arduino to the AVR C programming dialect on which it's based. Likewise, you can include AVR-C code specifically into your Arduino programs in the event that you need to.

• Open source and extensible equipment - The arrangements of the Arduino sheets are distributed under a Creative Commons permit, so experienced circuit creators can make their own variant of the module, augmenting it and enhancing it. Indeed, even generally unpracticed clients can manufacture the breadboard adaptation of the module with a specific end goal to see how it functions and spare cash.

Chapter 2

The Making of Arduino

Photograph: Randi Silberman Klett

The group as of late disclosed the Arduino Due, a board with a 32-bit Cortex-M3 ARM processor that offers all the more registering force for creators with complex tasks. Snap to amplify.

The beautiful town of Ivrea, which straddles the blue-green Dora Baltea River in northern Italy, is acclaimed for its underdog lords. In 1002, King Arduin turned into the leader of the nation, just to be deposed by King Henry II, of Germany, after two years. Today, the Bar di Re Arduino, a bar on a cobblestoned road around the local area, respects his memory, and that is the place an impossible new ruler was conceived.

The bar is the watering opening of Massimo Banzi, the Italian fellow benefactor of the hardware extend that he named Arduino to pay tribute to the place. Arduino is an ease microcontroller board that lets even a beginner do truly astonishing things. You can interface an Arduino to a wide range of sensors, lights, engines, and different gadgets and utilize simple to-learn programming to program how your creation will carry on. You can construct an intuitive show or a versatile robot and after that impart your plan to the world by posting it on the Net.

Discharged in 2005 as an unassuming device for Banzi's understudies at the Interaction Design Institute Ivrea (IDII), Arduino has generated a global do-it-without anyone's help insurgency in gadgets. You can purchase an Arduino board for pretty much US $30 or fabricate your own particular starting with no outside help: All equipment schematics and source code are accessible for nothing under open licenses. Subsequently, Arduino has turned into the most powerful open-source equipment development of now is the right time.

The little board is currently the go-to intend for specialists, specialists, understudies, and anybody with a gadgetry dream. More than 250 000 Arduino sheets have been sold the world over—and that does exclude the reams of clones. "It made it feasible for individuals do things they wouldn't have done something else," says David A. Mellis, who was an understudy at IDII before seeking after graduate work at the MIT Media Lab and is the lead programming engineer of Arduino.

There are Arduino-based breathalyzers, LED 3D shapes, home-computerization frameworks, Twitter shows, and even DNA examination packs. There are Arduino gatherings and Arduino clubs. Google has as of late discharged an Arduino-based improvement unit for its Android cell phone. As Dale Dougherty, the supervisor and distributer of Make magazine, the authoritative guide of DIY manufacturers, puts it, Arduino has turned into "the brains of producer undertakings."

However, Arduino isn't only an open-source extend that expects to make innovation more available. It's additionally a new business keep running by Banzi and a gathering of companions, and it's confronting a test that even their enchantment board can't tackle: how to survive achievement and develop. "We have to make the following hop," Banzi lets me know, "and turn into a built up organization."

Arduino ascended out of another impressive test: how to instruct understudies to make hardware, *q*uick. It was 2002, and Banzi, a hairy and avuncular programming modeler, had been brought on by IDII as a partner educator to advance better approaches for doing intuitive plan—an early field in some cases known as physical figuring. Be that as it may, with a contracting spending plan and restricted class time, his choices for instruments were few.

In the same way as other of his associates, Banzi depended on the BASIC Stamp, a microcontroller made by California organization Parallax that designers had been utilizing for about 10 years. Coded with the BASIC programming dialect, the Stamp resembled a clean little circuit board, pressing the fundamentals of a power supply, a microcontroller, memory, and information/yield ports for appending equipment. Yet, the BASIC Stamp had two issues, Banzi found: It didn't have enough figuring power for a portion of the tasks his understudies had at the top of the priority list, and it was additionally a bit excessively costly—a board in addition to essential parts could cost about US $100. He likewise required something that could keep running on Macintosh PCs, which were omnipresent among the IDII originators. Imagine a scenario where they could make a board that suited their needs themselves.

Banzi had an associate from MIT who had built up a creator agreeable programming dialect called Processing. Handling was quickly picking up prevalence since it permitted even unpracticed software engineers to make complex—and lovely—information representations. One reason for its prosperity was a to a great degree simple to-utilize coordinated improvement environment, or IDE. Banzi thought about whether they could make comparable programming apparatuses to code a microcontroller rather than design on a screen.

An understudy in the program, Hernando Barragán, made the primary strides in that course. He built up a prototyping stage called Wiring, which included both an easy to understand IDE and a prepared to-utilize circuit board. It was a promising task that proceeds right up 'til today, however Banzi was at that point thinking greater: He needed to make a stage that was considerably more straightforward, less expensive, and less demanding to utilize.

Photograph: Massimo Banzi

The principal model board, made in 2005, was a straightforward outline, and it wasn't called Arduino. Massimo Banzi would coin the name soon thereafter.

Photograph: Massimo Banzi

The Arduino group contracted with an organization that can produce from 100 to 3000 sheets for each day at an office close Ivrea, Italy. Snap to extend.

Banzi and his colleagues were solid adherents to open-source programming. Since the reason for existing was to make a snappy and effortlessly available stage, they felt they'd be in an ideal situation opening up the venture to whatever number individuals as could reasonably be expected instead of keeping it shut. Another element that added to that choice was that in the wake of working for a long time, IDII was coming up short on assets and would close its entryways. Employees dreaded their tasks would not survive or would be misused. "So we said, 'Overlook it,' " Banzi reviews. " 'How about we make it open source.' "

The open-source display had for **q**uite some time been utilized to fuel advancement for programming, yet not e**q**uipment. To make it work, they needed to locate a proper authorizing arrangement that could apply to their board. After some examination, they understood that on the off chance that they basically took a gander at their venture in an unexpected way, they could utilize a permit from Creative Commons, the not-for-profit assemble whose understandings are ordinarily utilized for social works, for example, music and composing. "You could consider e**q**uipment bit of culture you need to impart to other individuals," Banzi says.

To make the board, the gathering had a particular, understudy cordial cost as their objective: $30. "It must be what might as well be called going out to supper at a pizza put," Banzi says. They likewise needed to make it peculiar, something that would emerge and be cool-looking to intellectual nerds. On the off chance that different sheets were frequently green, they'd make theirs blue; while a few makers streamlined on information and yield pins, they'd add bounty to their board. As a last touch, they included a little guide of Italy on the back of the board. "A considerable measure of the plan decisions are bizarre for a genuine architect," Banzi says with a knowing snicker, "yet I'm not a genuine specialist, so I did it sillily!"

For one of the "genuine" specialists on the group, Gianluca Martino, the flighty, meatball-surgery way to deal with circuit load up configuration was edifying. Martino depicts it as "another state of mind about hardware," he says, "not in a building way, where you need to number cathodes, however a do-it-without anyone else's help approach."

The item the group made comprised of shoddy parts that could without much of a stretch be found if clients needed to assemble their own particular sheets, for example, the ATmega328 microcontroller. In any case, a key choice was to guarantee that it would be, basically, attachment and-play: something somebody could remove from a crate, connect to a PC, and utilize promptly. Sheets, for example, the BASIC Stamp required that DIYers spend for about six different things that additional to the aggregate cost. In any case, for theirs, a client could simply haul out a USB link from the board and associate it to a PC—Mac or PC—to program the gadget.

"The reasoning behind Arduino is that on the off chance that you need to learn gadgets, you ought to have the capacity to take in as you go from the very beginning, rather than beginning by learning polynomial math," says another individual from the group, broadcast communications build David Cuartielles.

The group would soon put that reasoning under serious scrutiny. They gave 300 clear printed circuit sheets to the IDII understudies with a straightforward order: Look up the get together guidelines on the web, fabricate your own board, and utilize it for something. One of the main tasks was a hand crafted wake up timer that dangled from the roof by a link. At whatever point you hit the rest catch, the clock would ascend tauntingly higher into the air until you simply needed to get up.

Before long other individuals caught wind of the sheets. What's more, they needed one. The principal client was a companion of Banzi's, who requested one unit. The venture was beginning to take off, yet one noteworthy thing was feeling the loss of—a name for their creation. One night over beverages at the neighborhood bar, it came to them: Arduino, much the same as the bar—and the lord.

Expression of Arduino rapidly spread on the web, with no showcasing or publicizing. At an opportune time, it pulled in the consideration of Tom Igoe, a teacher of physical registering at the Interactive Telecommunications Program at New York University and today an individual from the center Arduino group. Igoe had been instructing courses to nontechnical understudies utilizing the BASIC Stamp however was inspired by Arduino's elements. "They had the presumption that you didn't know gadgets and programming, that you would not like to design a whole machine to make sure you could program a chip—you could simply open up the board, press transfer, and it works," he says. "I was likewise inspired with the objective of a $30 value, which made it available. This was one of the key components for me."

In such manner, the achievement of Arduino owes a great deal to the earlier presence of Processing and Wiring. Those tasks gave Arduino one of its fundamental qualities: the easy to use programming environment. Before Arduino, coding a microcontroller carried with it a troublesome expectation to learn and adapt. With Arduino, even those with no past gadgets encounter accessed a formerly impervious equipment world. Presently, fledglings don't need to learn much before they can manufacture a model that really works. It's an intense development when the absolute most famous devices out there work as "secret elements" that are shut and patent ensured.

For Banzi, this is maybe the most imperative effect of Arduino: the democratization of building. "Fifty years prior, to compose programming you required individuals in white overskirts who knew everything about vacuum tubes. Presently, even my mother can program," Banzi says. "We've empowered many individuals to make items themselves."

Not all architects cherish Arduino. The more persnickety ones wail over the item to dumbing down item creation and flooding the specialist advertise with dreary products. Mellis, be that as it may, doesn't see the advancement as cheapening the part of the designer by any stretch of the imagination. "By giving a stage that gives the craftsman or originator a chance to get a little route in there, it makes it simpler for them to work with designers and say, 'This is the thing that I need to do,' " he says. "I don't believe it's supplanting the designer; it's simply encouraging that coordinated effort."

To fuel more prominent reception of Arduino, the group is investigating how to incorporate it all the more profoundly into the training framework, from review schools to universities. A few colleges, including Carnegie Mellon and Stanford, as of now utilize Arduino. Mellis has been contemplating how understudies and laypeople take to gadgets in a progression of workshops at the MIT Media Lab. Mellis welcomes 8 to 10 individuals to the lab, where they're given an assignment to finish through the span of a day. The undertakings have included building iPod speakers, FM radios, and a PC mouse utilizing a portion of similar segments that Arduino employments.

In any case, spreading the Arduino gospel is just part of the test. The group should likewise stay aware of interest for the sheets. Truth be told, the Arduino stage doesn't comprise of one sort of board any longer—there's presently a whole group of sheets. Notwithstanding the first plan, called the Arduino Uno, the new models incorporate an all the more intense board called the Arduino Mega, a conservative board called the Arduino Nano, a waterproof board called the LilyPad Arduino, and an as of late discharged, Net-empowered board called the Arduino Ethernet.

Arduino has additionally made its own particular house industry for DIY gadgets. There are more than 200 merchants of Arduino items around the globe, from substantial organizations, for example, SparkFun Electronics, in Boulder, Colo., to mother and-pop operations serving nearby needs. Banzi as of late got notification from a man in Portugal who quit his occupation at the telephone organization to offer Arduino items from his home. Arduino colleague Gianluca Martino, who directs creation and dissemination, says they're working additional time to achieve developing markets, for example, China, India, and South America. Now, he says, around 80 percent of the Arduino gathering of people is part between the United States and Europe, with the rest scattered the world over.

Since the group can't bear to stock countless sheets, they rather deliver anywhere in the range of 100 to 3000 every day at an assembling office close Ivrea. The group made a custom framework for testing the pins on every board, which for the Uno incorporates 14 advanced I/O pins, 6 simple info pins, and another 6 pins for the power supply—a major *q*uality-confirmation challenge when you're taking care of a large number of units a day. The Arduino board is sufficiently cheap for the group to guarantee to supplant any board that doesn't work. Martino says the disappointment rate is beneath 1 percent.

The Arduino group is presently ac*q*uiring enough to bolster two of its individuals as full-time representatives and is making arrangements to convey much more circuit load up energy to the general population. In September, at the Maker Faire, a tradition in New York City supported by Make magazine, the group propelled its first board with a 32-bit processor—an ARM chip—up from the 8-bit one of the past. This will serve the interest for fueling more vigorous peripherals. The MakerBot Thing-O-Matic, for instance, is a 3-D printer pack based on Arduino, yet it would profit by a speedier processor to accomplish more muddled assignments.

Arduino got another support this year when Google discharged an Arduino-based designer board for its Android framework. Google's Android ADK, or Accessory Development Kit, is a stage that gives an Android a chance to telephone connect with engines, sensors, and different gadgets. You can fabricate an Android application that uses the telephone's camera, movement sensors, touch screen, and Internet availability to control a show or robot, for instance. Aficionados say that the additional Android capacity opens up the conceivable outcomes for Arduino extends much more.

The group is mindful, be that as it may, about overcomplicating Arduino. "The test is figuring out how to suit all the diverse things that individuals need to do with the stage," Mellis says, "without making it excessively complex for somebody simply beginning."

Meanwhile, they're making the most of their far-fetched acclaim. Fans go from far away just to have a drink at the bar in Ivrea where the marvel got its name. "Individuals go to the bar and say, 'We're here as a result of the Arduino board,' " Banzi says. There's only one issue, he includes with a chuckle: The barkeeps don't comprehend what the Arduino board is.

Chapter 3

Arduino

Arduino Uno SMD R3

Arduino is an open-source PC equipment and programming organization, venture and client group that outlines and makes microcontroller-based units for building computerized gadgets and intuitive items that can detect and control protests in the physical world.

The venture depends on microcontroller board plans, fabricated by a few sellers, utilizing different microcontrollers. These frameworks give sets of computerized and simple I/O sticks that can be interfaced to different development sheets ("shields") and different circuits. The sheets highlight serial interchanges interfaces, including USB on a few models, for stacking programs from PCs. The microcontrollers are basically modified utilizing a vernacular of components from the C and C++ programming dialects. Notwithstanding utilizing conventional compiler toolchains, the Arduino extend gives an incorporated advancement environment (IDE) in view of the Processing venture.

The Arduino extend began in 2005 as a program for understudies at the Interaction Design Institute Ivrea in Ivrea, Italy, meaning to give an economical and simple path for amateurs and experts to make gadgets that interface with their surroundings utilizing sensors and actuators. Regular cases of such gadgets expected for apprentice specialists incorporate straightforward robots, indoor regulators, and movement locators.

Arduino sheets are accessible monetarily in preassembled frame, or as do-it-without anyone's help packs. The equipment outline determinations are straightforwardly accessible, permitting the Arduino sheets to be produced by anybody. Adafruit Industries evaluated in mid-2011 that more than 300,000 authority Arduinos had been economically delivered, and in 2013 that 700,000 authority sheets were in clients' grasp.

History

The root of the Arduino extend began at the Interaction Design Institute Ivrea in Ivrea, Italy. Around then understudies utilized a BASIC Stamp at a cost of $100, considered costly for understudies. In 2004, Colombian understudy Hernando Barragán made the improvement stage Wiring as a Master's theory extend at the Interaction Design Institute Ivrea (IDII) in Ivrea, Italy. Massimo Banzi and Casey Reas, who are known for work on the Processing dialect were chiefs for his postulation. The venture objective was to make ease, straightforward apparatuses for non-designers to make advanced undertakings. The Wiring stage comprised of an equipment PCB with an ATmega168 microcontroller, an IDE in light of Processing and library capacities to effortlessly program the microcontroller.

In 2005, Massimo Banzi, with David Mellis, an IDII , and David Cuartielles, included support for the less expensive ATmega8 microcontroller to Wiring. Be that as it may, rather than proceeding with the work on Wiring, they forked (or replicated) the Wiring source code and began running it as a different venture, called Arduino.

The Arduino's underlying center group comprised of Massimo Banzi, David Cuartielles, Tom Igoe, Gianluca Martino, and David Mellis.

The name Arduino originates from a bar in Ivrea, where a portion of the originators of the venture used to meet. The bar was named after Arduin of Ivrea, who was the margrave of the March of Ivrea and King of Italy from 1002 to 1014.

Taking after the consummation of the Wiring stage, lighter and lower cost renditions were circulated in the open-source group.

Equipment

Arduino-perfect R3 UNO board made in China with no Arduino logo, yet with indistinguishable markings, including "Made in Italy" content

Arduino is open-source equipment. The equipment reference plans are conveyed under a Creative Commons Attribution Share-Alike 2.5 permit and are accessible on the Arduino site. Format and generation records for a few variants of the equipment are likewise accessible. The source code for the IDE is discharged under the GNU General Public License, form 2. By the by an official Bill of Materials of Arduino sheets has never been discharged by the staff of Arduino.

In spite of the fact that the equipment and programming plans are uninhibitedly accessible under copyleft licenses, the designers have asked for that the name "Arduino" be select to the official item and not be utilized for determined works without authorization. The official strategy archive on utilization of the Arduino name stresses that the venture is interested in joining work by others into the official item. A few Arduino-perfect items economically discharged have maintained a strategic distance from the Arduino name by utilizing - duino name variations.

An early Arduino board with a RS-232 serial interface (upper left) and an Atmel ATmega8 microcontroller chip (dark, bring down right); the 14 advanced I/O pins are at the top, the 6 simple information pins at the lower right, and the power connector at the lower left.

An Arduino board comprises of an Atmel 8-, 16-or 32-bit AVR microcontroller (in spite of the fact that since 2015 other producers' microcontrollers have been utilized) with integral segments that encourage programming and consolidation into different circuits. A vital part of the Arduino is its standard connectors, which let clients interface the CPU board to an assortment of compatible extra modules named shields. A few shields speak with the Arduino board straightforwardly over different pins, however many shields are exclusively addressable by means of an I^2C serial transport—such a large number of shields can be stacked and utilized as a part of parallel. Before 2015, Official Arduinos had utilized the Atmel megaAVR arrangement of chips, particularly the ATmega8, ATmega168, ATmega328,

ATmega1280, and ATmega2560. In 2015, units by different makers were included. A modest bunch of different processors have likewise been utilized by Arduino perfect gadgets. Most sheets incorporate a 5 V straight controller and a 16 MHz precious stone oscillator (or artistic resonator in a few variations), albeit a few outlines, for example, the LilyPad keep running at 8 MHz and abstain from the installed voltage controller because of particular shape figure confinements. An Arduino's microcontroller is likewise pre-modified with a boot loader that streamlines transferring of projects to the on-chip streak memory, contrasted and different gadgets that ordinarily require an outside chip software engineer. This makes utilizing an Arduino more clear by permitting the utilization of a conventional PC as the developer. As of now, optiboot bootloader is the default bootloader introduced on Arduino UNO. At a calculated level, when utilizing the Arduino incorporated advancement environment, all sheets are modified over a serial association. Its usage shifts with the equipment adaptation. Some serial Arduino sheets contain a level shifter circuit to change over between RS-232 rationale levels and transistor–transistor rationale (TTL) level signs. Current Arduino sheets are modified by means of Universal Serial Bus (USB), executed utilizing USB-to-serial connector chips, for example, the FTDI FT232. A few sheets, for example, later-show Uno sheets, substitute the FTDI chip with a different AVR chip containing USB-to-serial firmware, which is reprogrammable by means of its own ICSP header. Different variations, for example, the Arduino Mini and the informal Boarduino, utilize a separable USB-to-serial connector board or link, Bluetooth or different strategies, when utilized with conventional microcontroller devices rather than the Arduino IDE, standard AVR in-framework programming (ISP) writing computer programs is utilized.

An authority Arduino Uno R2 with depictions of the I/O areas

The Arduino board uncovered the greater part of the microcontroller's I/O pins for use by different circuits. The Diecimila,

Duemilanove, and current Uno give 14 advanced I/O pins, six of which can create beat width adjusted signs, and six simple information sources, which can likewise be utilized as six computerized I/O pins. These pins are on the highest point of the board, by means of female 0.1-inch (2.54 mm) headers. A few module application shields are likewise financially accessible. The Arduino Nano, and Arduino-good Bare Bones Board and Boarduino sheets may give male header sticks on the underside of the board that can connect to solderless breadboards.

Numerous Arduino-perfect and Arduino-inferred sheets exist. Some are practically proportional to an Arduino and can be utilized reciprocally. Many upgrade the fundamental Arduino by including yield drivers, frequently for use in school-level training, to streamline making surreys and little robots. Others are electrically identical however change the shape calculate, in some cases holding similarity with shields, at times not. A few variations utilize distinctive processors, of differing similarity

Chapter 4

Official sheets

Additional data: List of Arduino sheets and perfect frameworks

The first Arduino equipment was delivered by the Italian organization Smart Projects. Some Arduino-marked sheets have been outlined by the American organizations SparkFun Electronics and Adafruit Industries. Starting 2016, 17 adaptations of the Arduino equipment have been industrially delivered.

-

Arduino RS232

(through opening parts)

- Arduino Diecimila

- Arduino Duemilanove

(rev 2009b)

- Arduino Uno R2

- Arduino Uno SMD R3

-

Arduino Leonardo

-

Arduino Pro

(No USB)

-

Arduino Mega

-

Arduino Nano

(Plunge 30 impression)

-

Arduino LilyPad 00

(rev 2007) (No USB)

-

Arduino Robot

-

Arduino Esplora

-

Arduino Ethernet

(AVR + W5100)

-

Arduino Yun

(AVR + AR9331)

•

Arduino Due

(ARM Cortex-M3 center)

Shields

Arduino and Arduino-perfect sheets utilize printed circuit extension sheets called shields, which connect to the ordinarily provided Arduino stick headers. Shields can give engine controls to 3D printing and different applications, Global Positioning System (GPS), Ethernet, fluid precious stone show (LCD), or breadboarding (prototyping). A few shields can likewise be made do it without anyone else's help (DIY).

Numerous shields can be stacked. In this case the top shield contains a solderless breadboard.

-

Dragino Lora Shield permits the client to send information and achieve greatly long ranges at low information rates.

-

Sink terminal breakout shield a wing-sort arrange

-

Adafruit Motor Shield with screw terminals for association with engines

-

Adafruit Datalogging Shield with a Secure Digital (SD) card opening and ongoing clock (RTC) chip

Programming improvement

Arduino Software IDE

Screenshot of the Arduino IDE demonstrating the Blink basic apprentice program

Arduino projects might be composed in any programming dialect with a compiler that produces twofold machine code. Atmel gives an advancement domain to their microcontrollers, AVR Studio and the more up to date Atmel Studio, which can be utilized for programming Arduino.

The Arduino extend gives the Arduino coordinated improvement environment (IDE), which is a cross-stage application written in the programming dialect Java.

It began from the IDE for the dialects Processing and Wiring. It was made for individuals with no significant information of hardware. It incorporates a code supervisor with elements, for example, sentence structure highlighting, support coordinating, cutting/sticking content, seeking/supplanting content and programmed space, and gives straightforward a single tick instrument to order and transfer projects to an Arduino board. It additionally contains a message region, a content reassure, a toolbar with catches for basic capacities and a progression of menus.

A program composed with the IDE for Arduino is known as an "outline". Representations are saved money on the improvement PC as documents with the record expansion .ino. Arduino Software (IDE) before 1.0 spared draws with the augmentation .pde.

The Arduino IDE underpins the dialects C and C++ utilizing extraordinary principles to sort out code. The Arduino IDE supplies a product library from the

Wiring venture, which gives numerous normal info and yield techniques. Client composed code just requires two capacities, for beginning the portray and the primary projects circle, that are arranged and connected with a program stub principle() into an executable cyclic official program with the GNU toolchain, additionally included with the IDE circulation. The Arduino IDE utilizes the program avrdude to change over the executable code into a content record in hexadecimal coding that is stacked into the Arduino board by a loader program in the board's firmware.

Programming

Control LED (red) and coordinated LED on Line 13 (green) on Arduino perfect board, made in China

A negligible Arduino C/C++ outline comprise of just two capacities:

• setup(): This capacity is called once when a portray begins after catalyst or reset. It is utilized to introduce factors and stick modes, and to instate some other libraries.

- loop(): After setup() is called, this capacity is called over and over. It controls the board until it is fueled off or is reset.

Most Arduino sheets contain a light-radiating diode (LED) and a heap resistor associated between stick 13 and ground, which is an advantageous component for some tests and program capacities. A run of the mill program for a starting Arduino developer flickers a LED more than once. This program is generally stacked in the Arduino by the maker. In the Arduino environment, a client may compose such a program as appeared:

```
#define    LED_PIN    13/Pin    number
appended to LED.


void setup() {
```

```
pinMode(LED_PIN,   OUTPUT);/Configure
stick 13 to be an advanced yield.


}


void circle() {


digitalWrite(LED_PIN,   HIGH);/Turn   on
the LED.


delay(1000);/Wait    1    second    (1000
milliseconds).


digitalWrite(LED_PIN, LOW);/Turn off the
LED.


delay(1000);/Wait 1 second.


}
```

This program utilizes the capacities pinMode(), digitalWrite(), and delay(), which are given by the interior libraries incorporated into the IDE environment.

Applications

• Xoscillo, an open-source oscilloscope

• Scientific hardware, for example, the Chemduino

• Arduinome, a MIDI controller gadget that impersonates the Monome

• OBDuino, an outing PC that uses the on-board diagnostics interface found in most present day autos

• Ardupilot, ramble programming and equipment

- ArduinoPhone, a do-it-without anyone else's help cellphone

- GertDuino, an Arduino mate for the Raspberry Pi

- Water *q*uality testing stage

- Homemade CNC utilizing Arduino and DC engines with close circle control by Homofaciens

- DC engine control utilizing Arduino and H-Bridge Acknowledgments

The Arduino extend got a privileged specify in the Digital Communities class at the 2006 Prix Ars Electronica.

Trademark debate

In mid 2008, the five fellow benefactors of the Arduino extend made an organization, Arduino LLC, to hold the trademarks connected with Arduino. The produce and offer of the sheets was to be finished by outer organizations, and Arduino LLC would get a sovereignty from them. The establishing local laws of Arduino LLC determined that each of the five originators exchange responsibility for Arduino brand to the recently shaped organization.

Toward the end of 2008, Gianluca Martino's organization, Smart Projects, alongside Microsoft, enlisted the Arduino trademark in Italy and kept this a mystery from alternate prime supporters for around two years. This was uncovered when the Arduino organization attempted to enroll the trademark in different ranges of the world (they initially enlisted just in the US), and found that it was at that point enlisted in Italy. Transactions with Gianluca and his firm to bring the trademark under control of the first Arduino organization fizzled. In 2014, Smart Projects started declining to pay sovereignties. They then named another

CEO, Mr. Musto, who renamed the organization to Arduino SRL and made a site named arduino.org, duplicating the design and format of the first Arduino.cc. This brought about a break in the Arduino advancement group. All Arduino sheets are still accessible to buyers so the ramifications of this are unverifiable.

In May 2015, "Genuino" was made far and wide as another trademark, held by Arduino LLC, and is at present being utilized as Arduino LLC's image name outside of the US.

At the World Maker Faire in New York on October 1, 2016, Arduino LLC prime supporter and CEO Massimo Banzi and Arduino SRL CEO Federico Musto declared that the 2 Arduino organizations will join and get to be distinctly one. From the Arduino Website: "Toward the end of 2016, the recently made "Arduino Holding" will turn into the single purpose of contact for the discount dispersion of all present and future items, and will keep on bringing enormous developments to the market.

Chapter 5

DIY Arduino-Based Sous-Vide Machine

Assemble your own one of a kind sous-vide machine and get flawlessly cooked suppers with high-accuracy temperature control. Get your Arduino, a rice cooker, and a temperature sensor and how about we begin.

Is it true that you are a foodie or essentially simply appreciate eating an appropriately cooked dinner? On the off chance that the answer is yes, you need a sous-vide machine in your life. They are anything but difficult to fabricate and keep up and the entire venture should be possible in only an end of the week. This venture is generally devoted to meat sweethearts, yet veggie lovers could likewise make utilization of this gadget.

What Is a Sous-Vide Machine?

As a matter of first importance, you might ponder what a sous-vide machine even is. The name isn't that natural on the off chance that you don't communicate in French (or regardless of the possibility that you do). "Sous vide" is French for "under vacuum", which gives an insight about its motivation.

Generally, step one is to put the sustenance to be cooked into a plastic pack and vacuum it shut. You then lower the pack into the machine, which is loaded with water warmed to an exact temperature. (As a note, you don't really need to completely vacuum pack the nourishment. You can simply put the sustenance into an open sack and lower its base half into the machine, permitting the weight of the water to expel the air around the nourishment.)

This is a culinary technique created to basically bubble nourishments, particularly meats, without losing juices or flavor into the water. In any case, what's the advantage? Wouldn't it be better (and less demanding) just to cook a steak in a skillet?

The answer is basically "no" and I'll explain to you why. We should assume that you make the most of your steak medium uncommon. When you cook it in a skillet, the meat isn't consistently cooked on the grounds that it is cooked from the outside in. This outcomes in the center being flawlessly cooked and pink, yet then moving more remote far from the inside it is more medium, and it may even be well done all things considered.

Presently, on the off chance that we cook a similar bit of steak in a sous-vide machine, the bit of meat would be consummately cooked completely through. Here is a photo to better comprehend what is going on:

On the off chance that you were not completely persuaded this venture was worth doing toward the starting, I trust this has altered your opinion. How about we stop here with the "why" and begin fabricating our sous-vide machine!

BOM

Above all else, for our sous-vide machine to be as basic as would be prudent, we will require a fundamental rice cooker. This contains our craved warmer and the holder for water. Right away, here is the total BOM:

• Rice cooker

• Arduino Nano

• LEG-5 hand-off

• 2.2kω resistor

• 2N2222 NPN transistor

- MCP9701* thermistor IC

- 1N400x diode

- Push catches (amount 3)

- 16×2 LCD with a Hitachi HD44780 I2C controller

- 5V control supply

- Extension line

- Epoxy**

- 100nF decoupling capacitor (prescribed, yet not basic)

*You could utilize a DS18B20 rather however you'd have to change the code in like manner

**For waterproofing the temperature sensor

The Hardware

We should now discuss the equipment part of this venture. Here is the schematic:

If you don't mind interface everything as you find in the schematic. Beneath I will attempt to clarify why we picked the particular segments and how they function.

MCU (Microcontroller Unit)

For the "brains" of this gadget, we will utilize an extremely essential advancement board: the Arduino Nano. It has the same microcontroller, ATMEGA328, as the Arduino Uno, yet in SMD shape.

LCD

The LCD is a typical 16×2 character show with a Hitachi HD44780 controller. Appended to it is an I2C board that likewise contains a potentiometer for differentiation alteration. I chose to utilize this since we will just need four pins to speak with our Arduino: two for information and two for power.

Hand-off

The LEG-5 hand-off is a through-opening segment that goes about as a switch, shutting when current is driven through the curl. You can utilize whatever other hand-off; simply ensure that the ostensible loop voltage is 5V and that it has an inductive AC contact rating no less than 1.5 circumstances more noteworthy than the current required by your rice cooker. For instance, my rice cooker needs around 2A AC, and the LEG-5 transfer has a rating of 3A.

In the schematic, there is additionally a diode in parallel (really, entirely, it is antiparallel) with the hand-off curl. This diode is called (among different names) a flyback diode, and it ensures the transistor by giving a way to the inductive current that keeps on streaming after the transistor is killed.

Another imperative part of this venture is the way to "take advantage of" the electrical string. (We're utilizing an electrical rope since we would prefer not to destroy the string connected to the rice cooker.) We have to make a break in one of the additional line wires and embed our transfer.

Family unit electrical links comprise of "line", "impartial", and "ground". With a specific end goal to appropriately kill on or the sous-vide machine, we have to embed a hand-off in the line conductor. We could put the hand-off in the impartial channel, however it is great practice to utilize the line transmitter since this approach can give additional assurance against electric stun. You can figure out which is the line wire by utilizing a mains analyzer (which generally resembles a screwdriver) or taking after the wiring shading codes particular to your nation. You can discover more about shading codes here. Another great practice is to utilize a twofold hand-off or two transfers to switch both the line and the impartial.

Essential note: When assembling this venture, be watchful with the mains voltage. Continuously ensure everything is unplugged when you are tinkering with the wires, and orchestrate the wiring to such an extent that it is inconceivable for the (uncovered) line and impartial directors to come into contact. On the off chance that you aren't 100% certain about what you are doing, please ask in the remarks or in the gathering before you proceed with your venture.

Proceeding with the exchanging part of the schematic, you can see that there is a NPN transistor and a resistor there. This is to open up the current expected to empower the loop of the hand-off. We require this in light of the fact that the current required by the hand-off (72 mA) is more prominent than what our microcontroller can yield (without a doubt the most extreme I/O-stick yield current is 40 mA, and normal working streams ought to be altogether lower). The resistor is expected to restrict the current going into the base of the transistor, which is proposed to work as a switch (i.e., in the immersion locale). You can read more about this subject here and here.

Catches

The switches are ordinary pushbutton switches that are shut just when they are squeezed (they don't keep up that state after discharge). We needn't bother with any outer draw up resistors since we will utilize the microcontroller's inside force ups. For more data on switch sorts, go here.

Temperature Sensor

The foundation of this venture is the temperature sensor, the MCP9701. I didn't pick this specific gadget for a particular outline reasons; it was exactly what I had accessible. It has better than average exactness, and the interface is direct—it yields a voltage (Vout) corresponding to the surrounding temperature (Ta), with an incline (Tc, i.e., Temperature Coefficient) of 19.5 mV/°C and a balance voltage (V0°C) of 400mV.

$$Vout=(Tc×Ta)+V0°C$$

I propose that while setting this sensor in the sous-vide, it ought to be in the focal point of the pot and at medium profundity, or possibly near the plastic pack that contains the to-be-cooked thing.

This temperature sensor is not waterproof, so we have to make it waterproof before we can utilize it for this venture. To do this, we bind wires to it and after that dunk it in epoxy so that any conductive part is secured. Here is the manner by which mine turned out:

My waterproofed temperature sensor

In the event that you would prefer not to experience this inconvenience, you can utilize an officially waterproofed sensor.

On the schematic, there is a decoupling capacitor, C1. My circuit functioned admirably without it, however it's a smart thought to incorporate it.

Control Supply

At long last, the power supply! One 5V supply is utilized for the whole circuit. You ought to discover something that can source no less than 150mA. For instance, a cell phone charger will carry out the occupation.

Programming

Since we are finished with the equipment, we should take a gander at the product.

You can see that there are two documents : "main.ino" and "main.h". The header document, with the expansion ".h", incorporates assertions for every one of the factors and constants utilized furthermore the "incorporate" orders, since we are utilizing two libraries, which you should introduce. The first is the PID library by Brett Beauregard, which will be utilized to control the transfer to acquire the fancied temperature, and the second one is a library for controlling the LCD by means of I2C. On the off chance that you wish to change parameters or what pins to utilize, you ought to do this in the header record.

In the "main.ino" record we locate the essential Arduino capacities "setup()" and "loop()". In setup() we instate every one of the factors that need a default esteem furthermore set the pins as either yield (for the transfer) or contribution (for the switches).

In the fundamental circle we call five capacities:

• cook(): We call this capacity just if the variable "begin" is set to "genuine" and if the passed time since the begin of cooking is not exactly the picked cooking time. Inside this capacity the "enchantment" happens. We read the temperature by means of the "read_temp()" capacity and we pass it to the PID controller, which will give us a yield. In light of this yield, we set the hand-off control stick to either "HIGH" or "LOW". A PID controller is a criticism framework that figures a yield esteem in light of the blunder, which is the distinction between the setpoint (our coveted temperature) and the present temperature, and three constants alluded to as P (relative), I (vital), and D (subsidiary). To take in more about PID control, investigate one of my past tasks, Do-It-Yourself Soldering Station with an ATmega8. In the sous-vide extend, we utilize the yield to control the "on time" of the transfer, in light of the fact that the hand-off must be on or off (2 values).

• checkBacklight(): This capacity confirms if any catch has been squeezed in the most recent 30 seconds. If not, it will kill the backdrop illumination.

• updateButtons(): Here, the present condition of the catches is checked.

• checkMenu(): Could likewise be known as the "menu work"; it utilizes numerous change explanations to explore around the menu and set the temperature and cooking time utilizing the three catches.

• updateDisplay(): Lastly, we upgrade the LCD to show the principle menu and parts of it or the present temperature and remaining cooking time (if the sous-vide cooking procedure is in progress).

• read_temp(): This one is not straightforwardly brought in the fundamental circle, but rather it is an essential capacity. It makes 5 readings before all else (in the setup() work) and after that, in the principle circle(), it subtracts the last perusing, includes another, and figures a normal. What this fundamentally does is smooth our info information. You can take in more about this on this Arduino page. The arrived at the midpoint of significant worth is then changed over to degrees Celsius utilizing the recipe introduced to you above in the "Temperature Sensor" area. We change over the perusing from the 10-bit ADC to millivolts, then we subtract 400 (the balance), and after that we isolate by the incline in mV/degree (i.e., 19.5) to acquire the temperature in degrees Celsius.

Utilizing a Customizable Interface Development Tool with Arduino

Advancement apparatuses that let you make intuitive interface devices for Arduino and Raspberry Pi undertakings are very mainstream. I got my hands on one to use in a remarkable science venture—here's the means by which it went.

A couple of months prior I was gone up against with an intriguing test. I instruct at a STEM-arranged after-school club and an understudy clarified that he was making bismuth precious stones and required help with a to some degree one of a kind issue.

In the event that you don't recall from science class (I didn't), bismuth is a component, nuclear number 83. It is a silver-shaded, delicate metal which is strong yet fragile at room temperature. In the event that you soften it down and after that let it cool, it will frame precious stones. Because of oxidation, the gems will go up against some amazing hues, from pink to green to blue. My understudy was making the gems and offering them, yet needed an approach to screen and record the temperature of the metal as it warmed and cooled. Along these lines, on the off chance that he got a gem he enjoyed, he could endeavor to repeat it.

Some time later, we had two or three Python scripts that would screen the temperature, showing it as a line diagram on the PC screen and recording it to a CSV petition for future reference. It wasn't pretty, however it worked. From that point forward, I've backtracked and supplanted the greater part of our untidy code with a solitary program: MegunoLink.

What Does It Do?

MegunoLink is a truly cool program that permits you to make an on-screen interface for your venture. It's perfect with pretty much any board that has a serial association with the PC, including most Arduino sheets and the Raspberry Pi. It can interface over USB, UDP arrange associations, and the XBee Series 2.

For my situation, I am basically utilizing an Arduino Uno, alongside a photoresistor I had lying around.

My photoresistor setup

MegunoLink is, basically, a more astute variant of the serial screen in the Arduino IDE. It peruses all correspondences originating from the board and can send messages back. With MegunoLink, in any case, you introduce every line of data with a unique label which tells the PC what the numbers and content in that line mean.

You make a snappy intuitive format on screen, made up of different "boards". You can utilize anything from straightforward serial screens to a couple of various types of charts, or even maps if your board is passing GPS organizes.

MegunoLink then takes that data and, in light of the tag, sends it to the right "board" on screen. Sound muddled? No anxiety. In case you're utilizing Arduino, they have a library with a group of pre-made capacities to make the procedure snappy and simple.

Code

A program set up for MegunoLink is practically the same as what you may use for whatever other venture. Take note of that I made a "TimePlot" protest and that, rather than printing to Serial, I utilized the capacities from the MegunoLink library.

```
#include "MegunoLink.h"


int tmpsns = A1;


TimePlot tempPlot("tmp");


void setup() {
```

```
pinMode(tmpsns, INPUT);


Serial.begin(115200);/pick your most
loved baud rate!


}


void circle() {


int tempRead =
analogRead(tmpsns);/read sensor


tempPlot.SendData("Temp",
tempRead);/send information to plot


delay(100);
}
```

Perusing Outputs from a Project

Transfer your code, dispatch MegunoLink, then simplified a couple boards to get things how you need them. To get a few information that would be worth taking a gander at, I just waved my hand around over the sensor a bit.

Among our boards for this venture, we have a fundamental serial screen. Take note of the way that the information is labeled.

In the event that you needed to swear off the gave library, or in the event that you were utilizing an alternate gadget, you would simply utilize a typical serial print proclamation to send these messages (where the number toward the end of every line is the genuine perusing from the sensor and whatever is left of the line is the labels for MegunoLink).

From that information, MegunoLink builds a basic time plot. I exited the vast majority of the settings at their defaults, yet for all intents and purposes everything about this plot is adjustable, from the marks and breaking points on the tomahawks to the shades of the plot and the states of the focuses. You can zoom and container or even fare the information to a CSV document with one of the catches at the top.

In the event that you require, you can even handle more than one diagram at once, whether you need them in particular boards or overlaid in a similar board. You can likewise utilize the labels on the information to guide the data to a table, to a particular serial screen, or to a standard x,y plot (you would, obviously, need to supply the esteem for both tomahawks).

Giving Input to a Project

You can likewise do some cool stuff utilizing MegunoLink as a contribution for your venture. You can include an interface board, drag catches, sliders, drop boxes, checkboxes, names, content boxes, advance bars—and so on. You can then indicate what every control does by characterizing a string for it to send over serial.

For instance, I made a board with three catches.

Every catch sends a basic message—for instance, "red", "blue" and "green"— and my Arduino is customized to listen for those messages on the serial line. When one is gotten, it finishes a particular activity. For this situation, these messages flip a LED of the suitable shading. I had a great deal of fun with this one, including connecting a robot arm with catches and sliders to control each of its joints. The are heaps of conceivable outcomes.

Obviously, the program isn't suited for each application. In case you're simply squinting a light, MegunoLink might be more multifaceted nature than your venture needs. It's additionally just perfect with Windows and requires a touch of establishment, yet it does its employment well. In case you're searching for a less demanding approach to peruse information from or send contribution to your Arduino or Raspberry Pi extend, MegunoLink could be a solid match for you.

Streak Freeze Photography with an Arduino

Solidify minutes so as to effectively create exceptional close-up pictures with your computerized camera, an Arduino, and these basic circuits.

I have dependably been awed by fast photography. The photographic catch of what regularly goes inconspicuous, or possibly unnoticed, is interesting and intermittently lovely. Fast cameras, be that as it may, are costly and past the range of a considerable lot of us.

You can, notwithstanding, draw near to rapid photography utilizing a basic and modest method. In this venture, we will manufacture two straightforward and cheap circuits that, alongside your DSLR camera, a slave streak, and an Arduino

Uno, can duplicate a portion of the qualities of rapid photography to catch irregular minutes in time.

Prerequisites:

• Digital camera with manual concentration and capacity to set long presentation times

• External (slave) streak unit (see content)

• Hot shoe with outer terminal capacity and a link (see content)

• Arduino Uno

• One or both of the circuits introduced here (see Bill of Materials for each underneath)

Essential Technique

The "mystery" to this strategy is straightforward. To start with, physically center your camera. At that point, set your camera presentation to a moderately long esteem, say 4-6 seconds, and in entire or almost total dimness, take a photo. Commonly, these conditions will create an absolutely dark picture. Amid the long introduction time frame, be that as it may, the blaze will fire and give the main brightening amid the presentation. A brief minute caught by the glimmer.

The total FSR interface circuit on a breadboard with an Arduino Uno

The key is to control the terminating of the glimmer. In this venture, we will utilize an Arduino Uno to flame an outer glimmer when a particular outside occasion is detected. Any outside sensor can be utilized as the trigger occasion for the glimmer. Here, we will utilize two sensors, a compel detecting resistor and a sound sensor, to distinguish the outside occasion of intrigue.

Camera

The camera that I utilized for this venture is a Canon EOS 400D (Digital Rebel XTi). This is a moderately low-end (and, now, generally old) advanced SLR (single focal point reflex) camera. Any camera with a manual concentration and the capacity to set long exposures ought to work. Likewise with any nearby up photography, you require a focal point that can center at the wanted separation.

Streak Unit

The PL-ASF18 slave streak unit

We need the Arduino to trigger the blaze, so we require an outer glimmer unit. I utilized a Polaroid PL-ASF18 slave streak unit, presented previously. This is one of the most minimal evaluated slave streak units around and it works great. One specific favorable position is that it can be activated with a moderately low voltage (<6 V). (Other activating guidelines utilize higher voltages.) For the circuit that tails, it is important that you utilize an outside glimmer that acknowledges a low-voltage streak trigger.

The PL-ASF18 is very solid for close-up work, yet it works from two 1.5 V AA batteries. You will probably need to ricochet the glimmer to the objective as opposed to point it specifically at the objective. For the shots in this article, I didn't point the blaze unit specifically at the objective; rather, the glimmer was pointed straightforwardly far from the objective, and the light achieved the objective by reflecting off a bit of dark cardboard. Moreover, I utilized a light diffuser (a white nylon sheet tent) for a few shots. On the off chance that you have a unit with variable glimmer control that can be arranged remotely (the PL-ASF18 does not have that capacity), you might have the capacity to achieve a similar impact by decreasing the power.

Hot Shoe

Hot shoe with 3.5 mm attachment

The outer glimmer unit associates with a hot shoe, which is a fairly institutionalized "attachment" for a blaze unit. I utilized the one presented above (accessible here), which contains various shoes. All the more vitally, this hot shoe has a helpful 3.5 mm attachment where you generally observe the basic PC Sync connector. That connector externalizes the middle contact and the shoe mount—when shorted, the association will work the blaze. Most any hot shoe with the "standard" PC Sync connector (case here) will do likewise. The upside of this hot shoe, notwithstanding, is that the 3.5 mm attachment is exceptionally regular, just like the mating jack.

Notwithstanding which sort of connector you utilize, you will likewise need to make a link with the two leads from the hot shoe for appending to our circuit. You should recognize the positive and negative leads utilizing a voltmeter for right association. You will likewise need to gauge the voltage between these contacts to ensure that the voltage used to work the glimmer is inside the cutoff points of our circuit (see advance clarification beneath). The hot shoe, with the glimmer unit appended, can be mounted on a small scale tripod to encourage situating.

Compel Sensing Resistor

Interlink 406 drive detecting resistor

The Arduino needs to screen some outside occasion with a specific end goal to work the blaze at the sought time. The outer occasion for this variant of the venture is constrain, which we will gauge utilizing an Interlink 406 compel detecting resistor (PDF). The constrain detecting resistor (FSR) is presented above and is accessible from Adafruit and different sources. You can download the incorporation manage connected from this page for extra data on the sensor.

The resistance between the leads of this sensor shifts as per the drive applied upon its surface. That is, whether you drop a little *q*uestion at first glance or tap on it, the resistance will change. The Arduino will utilize this trademark to detect an outside occasion and trigger the blaze.

The leads from the FSR ought to be appended to a link to associate with our circuit. As specified in the combination manage connected above, to abstain from harming the FSR, don't straightforwardly patch to the leads. Rather, utilize female jumper drives, which can be pleated somewhat to give a tight fit.

Schematic for the FSR-Based System

Schematic for the Arduino interface to the FSR and blaze unit.

The schematic above is for the whole circuit that permits the Arduino UNO to screen the FSR and trigger the outer blaze. The circuit has three unmistakable parts: top, center, and base.

Best—External Flash Unit

The top segment permits the Arduino to control the outside glimmer unit. A rationale high flag on stick D2 will enact the LED inside the 4N25 optoisolator. The NPN transistor in the 4N25 will then turn on.

The authority and emitter terminals of the 4N25 are associated, individually, to the positive and negative terminals of the glimmer trigger (the blaze trigger associations originate from the link connected to the hot shoe attachment). Subsequently, when the LED is stimulated by the Arduino, the glimmer will be activated.

Take note of that the glimmer unit is electrically disengaged from the Arduino, and that is alluring. You should first *q*uantify the voltage at the terminals of the blaze unit (i.e., on the leads originating from the hot shoe link) to recognize the positive and negative terminals and to verify that you are not surpassing the most extreme authority to-emitter furthest reaches of the optoisolator. On the off chance that you have the leads turned around or the voltage surpasses the predefined most extreme, you will probably broil the optoisolator.

For the Motorola 4N25 that I utilized, the most extreme authority to-emitter voltage is 30 V, however not all optoisolators stamped 4N25 are the same, and you ought to counsel the producer's datasheet to decide the point of confinement for your segment. I quantified this voltage for the PL-ASF18 unit with crisp batteries and it was ~5.5 V, which is well underneath the most extreme. Yet, as of now said, diverse glimmer units can utilize distinctive trigger voltages, so measure the voltage first.

Center—Force-Sensing Resistor and Op Amp

The center of the schematic contains the FSR interface and employmentsa MCP601P operation amp (PDF). It is in no way, shape or form important to utilize this correct operation amp; the MCP601P was picked on the grounds that it is intended for single-supply operation and components a rail-to-rail yield. The MCP601P is utilized as a part of a comparator setup, with the end goal that it capacities as a limit switch.

The transforming contribution to the MCP601P is encouraged by a voltage divider framed by R3 and the FSR. R3 is 47 kω and was worked well in the circuit over the low end of the force–resistance bend, as appeared in Figure 10 of the previously mentioned FSR reconciliation direct.

Picture politeness of Interlink Electronics

The non-upsetting contribution to the MCP601P is likewise nourished by a voltage divider from the wiper of R4, a 200 kω multi-turn potentiometer. Altering the potentiometer changes the measure of constrain required to create a trigger flag from the operation amp.

The yield of the MCP601P goes to an Arduino computerized input port (D3). At the point when no compel is applied on the FSR, the yield of the operation amp ought to be 5 V—read by the Arduino advanced contribution as a rationale high. At the point when drive is applied on the FSR, its resistance will diminish, bringing on an expansion in the yield voltage of the FSR/R3 divider. Inevitably the voltage at the reversing information will surpass the voltage at the non-altering info, and this will drive the operation amp's yield voltage to ground. At the point when the Arduino recognizes this rationale low flag on stick D3, it triggers the glimmer unit.

R2 is a hysteresis resistor, implying that it smothers spurious yield moves. This is not entirely required on the grounds that, when a solitary trigger is recognized, the blaze unit is actuated, and a few seconds are required before the glimmer can be activated once more. It's for the most part great practice, be that as it may, to incorporate this resistor for a more controlled and unsurprising circuit. See this plan note (PDF) for a more entire depiction of hysteresis in a comparator circuit. Additionally, take note of that the circuit breadboarded for this venture could work viably without C1, yet it is great practice to incorporate a power-supply decoupling capacitor for both simple and computerized ICs.

Base—Input Switch

The base of the schematic essentially contains a flitting switch associated with a computerized input (D4) of the Arduino. The information will be perused by the Arduino as rationale low when not squeezed and rationale high when squeezed. We will utilize this switch contribution to the product to "arm" the blaze unit; after this, the program will sit tight for the trigger occasion.

BOM for the Arduino Interface to the FSR and Flash Unit

Component Description

C1 0.1 μF capacitor

R1 330 Ω resistor

R2 470 kω resistor

R3 47 kω resistor

R4 200 kω multi-turn potentiometer

R5 10 kω resistor

IC1 4N25 optoisolator

IC2 MCP601P operation amp

FSR1 FSR 406 constrain detecting resistor

SW1 momentary switch

Programming

The Arduino programming used to work the circuit, ImpactFlash.ino, is incorporated underneath. It is generally short and ought to be straightforward.

Basically, the product sits tight for SW1 to be squeezed. At the point when this happens, the Arduino's locally available LED is lit, showing the "equipped" state. At that point the product sits tight for a change from "high" to "low" on the trigger information.

At the point when a trigger flag is gotten, the glimmer unit is worked. In the event that you'd like, you can embed a short postponement after the trigger and before the blaze is worked. At times your photographic target will require a couple of milliseconds of deferral. After glimmer operation, the locally available LED squints for a programmable timeframe, amid which the blaze unit energizes. After that interim, the code again sits tight for SW1 to be squeezed.

You can set the variable DEBUG to 1 keeping in mind the end goal to get content yield to the serial screen at different focuses in the program. As a matter of course, DEBUG = 0, since the program is probably going to be utilized as a part of a remain solitary design, yet the serial screen yield can help you to pick up recognition with the program or to test the program in the wake of changing a few parameters.

Conclusion

Thank you again for downloading this book!

I hope this book was able to help you to UNDERSTAND what ARDUINO is all about and what it's meant for.

Finally, if you enjoyed this book, then I'd like to ask you for a favor, would you be kind enough to leave a review for this book on Amazon? It'd be greatly appreciated!

Thank you and good luck!

I truly do appreciate it!

Best Wishes,

Lee Maxwell

www.ingramcontent.com/pod-product-compliance
Lightning Source LLC
Chambersburg PA
CBHW060948050326
40689CB00012B/2601